Of Here And Hereafter

PETER BONNERJEE

BookLeaf Publishing
India | USA | UK

Presentation by *BookLeaf Publishing*

Web: www.bookleafpub.com

E-mail: info@bookleafpub.com

ISBN: 9789363313569

First edition 2024

DEDICATION

I dedicate the poems to my wife, Joyce.

"White was the color of your wedding dress,
and the shimmering glow of your face,
white, too, was the color of your coffin,
and the flowers that adorned your grave."

from "A Tribute"

ACKNOWLEDGEMENT

I acknowledge the inspiration I received from:
i. My Parents;
ii. The Jesuits;
iii. The House of Tata;
iv. My well-wishers: my six siblings; Dhruv and Aasha; Nanhe; Rita and Luluda; Rubydi and Anilda; Raju and Pamu; Eva and Shamim Bhai; Anjana; Shazia and Tabrez; Agnes and John; Ram Basu; my friends in Moitree; Maryam, my poet friend; Prabhat and Alka; and Prof. Sahab; and
v. BookLeaf Publishing.

PREFACE

Poetry, for me, is the expression of the soul, in relationship with others, in the universe. In poetry, therefore, I experienced the need for two essential elements: the freedom to be and a holistic worldview of existence.

Coming from a Biblical background, I found the understanding of the soul, the universe, and existence to be very meaningful and integrated—even though quite tumultuous. The imperfections in existence, I realized, lie not in the imperfections in the creation of the universe, but in the imperfections of immoral choices of human beings—the souls.

That understanding, however, was not easy to achieve. It involved years of contemplative reading of the major Holy Scriptures, philosophies, theoretical physics, and management thoughts. The output: bouts of depression and, finally, the joy of having understood existence.

PREFACE

THE STRUGGLING YEARS

Poetry is the yearning of the soul
in manifesting himself

I Believe

I will not dwell on broken dreams, as does
the autumn breeze over leafless branches.
Life has cast shadows
over my soul too long.
I would rather be the sun-scorched desert
that withers the idle thought,
than the trailing shadows of the jungle
where years of restless youth brood in solitude.

They say no man is forever,
no dream is for keeps;
yet over a soil I've lived and toiled,
I'll pick my staff again.
And in the morrows, I'll make for you
a gentle song for your restless sleep,
and in your pain, I'll give to you
my shoulders for your wounded dreams.

Tomorrow, I know,
I will not dwell on broken dreams.
Tomorrow, I know,
I'll come across a new belief.
For my tomorrow
will not be the wanton gift of todays—
with this blood of mine, verily,
I'll birth the dawn of tomorrow.

Tata's[1] Dream

Shadows lengthen over the road
as evening nestles deeper into night's embrace.
In the hazy interlude of light and darkness
man shies from earth's reality: pain for joy.
Over broken fields and jagged boulders
shadows lengthen the shawl of darkness
in a deceptive show of evenness.

Yet through those beguiling shadows
man must strive forward,
though bent by age and the sky overcast;
for far away a siren would beckon
where he must light,
like a diya[2] upon the altar,
molten steel in the heart of a furnace.

And for a moment, the shadows
in the flame of man's commitment
shall erupt into a joyful hue—
that tomorrow's generation
may seek through the shadows
light from today's worship.

***

Note: 1. Jamshetji Nussarwanji Tata, founder of the House of Tata and the steel industry in India.
2. Earthen lamp.

Man

Shall I tell him that time begins
where the age of puppy love ends;
or that the age of puppy love
begins the unfolding of a sprawling tree?
Shall I tell him that tulips and tears
adorn a woman,
whereas man is brawn;
or that it is fire and steel
and tears of failure
that mold a generation?

They say man is a pygmy
in the ocean of time—
an illegible scrawl
defying the sky.
Yet, whence was time
that man's destiny was not?
Like an indomitable will
begetting an urge to manifest perfection,
before the pain of Crucifixion is forgotten
the roar of his Resurrection begins!

Tell him, then, if you would—
that time binds no man
but keeps him on the rail;

that in man is life,
and that never was time
that the Man[1] was not!

***

Note: 1. The Crucifer and the Word of God.

Walking through Summer

My spirit squirms in this noose of flame
and the world around me gasps for breath,
like a crescendo of restlessness
instilling waves of endless agony.
Lord! What the hell's heaven like?
Is it a tale of songs and shadows,
where the spirit is laid in eternal rest?
Take me, Lord, to this abode
take me once, a night away,
from this living hell I call my home!

But fly me back to this woebegone,
that afterwards, when I've met the rain,
its soft caress on my simmering brain,
I'll tell you a tale of a joy-in-pain,
and you'll say—
"Oh, take me once to your Summer Rain!"

***

Rose in my Garden

In a meadow of green
all my own,
is a beautiful garden
there I have sown;
and the flowers I grow
are of every shade,
pink, scarlet, orange, yellow
in a fair and true cascade.
Some chrysanthemum, lily, dahlia
some marigold,
and others of variety and class
your eyes can't hold.

There the sun rays play
in the dew at morn,
and the moonbeams caress
the child bud born.
There the summers flow by
and the winters sigh,
the autumns sway along
as the springs come nigh.
Through all those years
and days gone by,
my Eden of green blooms
through the day and night.

But in the farthest corner
of my haven of green,
is a Tree of Rose
you may have seen;
for ‘midst that tree
where my longings flow,
are my years of barren—
the hope for a Rose.
But though the summers flow here
and the springs embrace,
yet in my bed of thorns
no Rose ever grace.

Alone in that solitude
I lie in wait,
to the thorns, I bleed
and my joys forsake;
yet my heart attends
as my soul encase,
the curse that surrounds me
I alone must face.
With my blood, I toil
and ever veer from my fate,
I’ll win, I know one day
but for now, I must wait…

***

At Crossroads

The evening spangled in streaks
of lush red, coral and pink,
as if the creative joy smeared the world
with a touch of joy.
But in the next moment
from the farthest cloud
came a spell of darkness
over the illumined sky.
And amidst that turbulence, the wind gathered
surging through the peepal leaves,
like a magic piper wielding a magic dream—
"Come, fly with me!"

Yet the leaves stayed on,
as if my imprisoned world
bade them so.
Like the wind last evening
that had lain frivolously
against your cascading hair,
sweeping it high
like a tidal wave.
Yet, even that windswept joy
couldn't span across our mutilated path—
as you passed me by
and I turned away.

So often generations pass us by
casually drifting through life,
and, like the fiery Apostles
now stone-lipped on Peter’s Basilica,
we merely stand and watch—
while the wind sows and reaps,
unable to touch.

***

Through the Window Bars

The outside world of laughing wind
surge in through the naked bars,
and for a moment's joy I know
an eagle's thrill in the open sky.

Somewhere in the whorls of time
where the curtains of Life would ruffle
and curious flames of summer dawn
peep into the dungeons of naked pain,
I pray the sunshine kisses away
the scars of loneliness of a longing dream.

Maybe then in the whorls of darkness
I would know,
that time is not stagnant really—
that someday
my whisper of dream will bloom
in the warm embrace of a womb.

***

Now at Summer

The dying strands of summer breeze
remind me of the hungry passion
that meets the first rain
on thirsty fields;
like the dim echoes
of an even at autumn
bring across the memory
of a fire that once was.

Maybe that is why
the summer must come—
to bring to me the thirst
That's you!

***

Nostalgia

The shriveled ancient sits
cradling his memory in solitude
of a tumultuous youth gone by;
while the wind outside
dances frivolously in the summer sky—
disdainful of a lingering cloud,
now bereft of rain,
clinging hard to her once fertility.

***

Carnival Night

Laughing faces, bashful faces,
leering faces, gazelle faces,
tens and scores of nameless faces;
caught in a maze of blazing lights
of blaring hawkers
and screaming children;
swirling in a maddening blasé
of flaming colors
and twirling trinkets—
like a sun-kissed spring
gushing through a rock-strewn bed
deafening the world stranded without—
whirling through the giant wheels,
oblivious as the night recedes
deeper into Aurora's sky;
spellbound over jesters in gaiety,
of stone-faced deities
reigning over bowed-down wistfulness,
of castes and creeds and languages
hand clasped and trailing behind
footsteps of peace and goodwill.

Life rolls along
stumbling through the mire
of procrastination,
and out of the torrid years

comes a night of laughter—
Why then for a night only?

***

The Marauder

Then the twilight departed...
leaving behind the weary world
to the company of descending darkness,
captivated by the song of crickets
and the flickering flame of fireflies.
And as the world snuggled deeper
into the arms of a restful sleep,
the silent marauder slides forth—
his shadow lengthening
over the monsoon grass.
Where youthful innocence
in the evening
played with abandoned gaiety,
now treads the soundless footfalls
of savagery and greed.
Stands alone as a witness
the dimly lit street lamps
squinting through the wet peepal leaves
and the melancholy blast
of a policeman on the beat.

Some hours from now,
with the bashful flush
of the Eastern sky,
will come the tide
of yet another dawn;

and peering through the rush
of factory workers
and morning strollers
will be the silent laughter
of last night's marauder.

***

Over a Table of Carolina[1]

The balls—
red, pink, green, brown,
brown, green, pink, red,
green, red, brown, pink,
pink, brown…
drawing in incessant monotony,
like waves crashing on the sea
in endless staccatos of ebbs and tides.

The players—
like robots
straining in mechanized stance,
as the cue strikes and the ball rolls,
one strikes another and another strikes another…
hating for hate, loving for love,
black is black,
white is white.

The lampshade—
stooping down on faces
motionless; for the wires stretch it taut.
Life, woven in timeless servility…
the drunkard to his wine,
the priest to his gods,
and the poet to his dream.
Existence in emptiness.

The smoldering cigarette—
living through its hour of agony
yet yearning for the boundless sky
through the crystal panes;
and at the last end,
in a desperate surge for immortality,
blazes into an irascible glow
before receding silently into smoke and ashes.

Outside on the street,
the sound of a sharp creak
is gobbled gleefully in the rush for survival—
unmindful of two starving bullocks,
strapped to the cart and the master's whip,
staggering painfully over a burdened climb.
Unmindful, too, is the apathy within,
as the game of Carolina rolls on…

***

Note: 1. A game in Billiards.

Roses for Merwyn

The night shall be peaceful
after a weary noon;
sleep well, my friend
no thirst shall wake your dream.
You have bid me goodbye
when I was miles away,
and when I met you again—
there were tears strewn around you
and wilted roses on your grave.

I have come to you in barren
to play the last command,
for death has won the race
and now the living moves along.
We have had our springs, my friend
we have had our winters, too,
we have had our share of glory
until the curtains drew.

Life had been a melody
for two on the roads to sing,
where words had been our searching
and years, the unfolding truth.
You have had your share of singing
you can sing no more with me,
my peace be yours

your pain be mine—
what can I wish you more!

***

Thirsty Noon

Tomorrow when I'm gone,
when the tide of time
will have withered my flame,
how will my impotence nourish you?
So come now—
while the lotus blooms,
while the summer yearns
and I thirst.

I have sought you
in the dew-filled petals of the dawn,
in the virgin freshness of the lily,
in the warm embrace of the winter noon.
And as at evening, the twilight bends
to engulf in the captive of the night,
I have sought you
in the voiceless darkness of anguish,
that holds me captive
enshrined in loneliness.

***

Good Friday

Lead me to the road
of gentle breeze
and pink carnations,
for I'm a man beset in darkness,
alive only to the drums of my dreams.
And if you see me falter,
hold me not, O Gentle Jew,
for I'm weary—
weary of the miles of Calvary
life has in store for me.

I've heard of the Mighty Paradise
stoop down
to build this clod of earth
a shelter from the storms—
Yet, they spat on his face.
Let man then,
for he so chose,
bury in the sands of his Frankenstein:
a befitting epitaph
to his decadent ways!

***

Muharram

The hour is breathless tonight
with distant echoes of muffled drums
and fragment sprays of anguished cries—
for tonight is Muharram,
the sacrificial night.

Tonight I shall thirst
on the sands of Karbala;
tonight I shall bleed
on the hills of Golgotha;
tonight I shall dance
on the snows of Kailash.
O heart, O heart,
I weep tonight
for the innocents
that have wilted in sorrow.
O Soul of my soul—
in pain, I searched for your love,
in despair, your wisdom,
and against tyranny
your sword of asunder.

Bear with me, O Anguished Night,
for tonight is the hour
of an age gone by.
Over the buried age

let me pledge tonight—
that for those crucified dreams
I shall stake my life.

***

Barren Sky

The night is alive
to so many dreams,
to so many promises
waiting at the doorstep,
like a sprinter at the starting point
straining for the whistle to blow;
but then swift like a spear,
piercing through the night
the pain of rejection
awakens;
as if to remind
the omnipotence of pain—
that life is pain,
that death is pain,
and that pain is the essence
of Existence itself.

So let it be:
in the fathomless pit
of that Dark Guile
let them sink—
those hundreds of hundreds
who refuse to heed our pleas;
but seek, instead, hope
beneath a barren sky.

***

Winter Song

The dusk is nigh
the chill wind blows,
those old and weary
to their homes must go;

Their hour is past
for the light has waned,
their limbs can no longer
shoulder the weight;

They must leave for the morrow
for the greens to enshrine—
for the night would be dreary
now that winter is nigh!

***

Tulips on Barren

I know a world beneath my feet
when through the lush open fields
I walk in hand with your name;
like the august sun above
in hand with the clouds
looking down on the creatures below.

But when in the dim-lit twilight
I walk, my feet penetrate
the silence of time;
and in that momentous time, I know
that like the Earth that shelters me,
I would rather be a healing touch
to the numerous broken souls.

***

In Nature

Alive am I
for Nature breathes
in every vein of my soul.
In every patter of rain
that dances upon silent stones,
and in every sway of breeze
that glides through the sesame leaves,
I hear the Song of Life.
In every dew-filled flower
that greets the sun at dawn,
and in every swirling wave
that floods over thirsty shores,
I see death falter.

O, Death—
harry me not with your barren calls;
go call the weary
that await your call:
for I am in Nature,
the Womb of Existence!

***

Alone amidst Uncertainty

The eyes look for inspiration
when the mind is in search,
sometime in the embers of a dying flame,
sometime in the floods of a torrential rain;
the eyes unravel,
the mind snaps it up.
So often in a solitary walk
through a maze of conflicting thoughts
despair descends,
and knowledge of a thousand generations,
caught in a clash of interpretations,
uninvited attends.

Unseen to the probing eyes
the mind stops to rest;
but barely it begins to resume
the flesh derails.
And in that moment
of life's endless struggle,
the soul flits out—
across barriers of limited reasoning
in search of the unknown "I AM."

Stands alone amidst that uncertainty
Faith—

unwavering, watchful, waiting…

***

THE CONTEMPLATIONS

As I journeyed through the night—
friends came out with their lamps
to guide me through the void
towards my home…

A Peep into the Unknown

A Vision

I gazed into the pool of Life
and beheld a silent, peaceful flow,
a water embedded in a sea so deep
with rippling waves that frolic in glee.

My pebbly thought
drops into the water
and erupts a thousand
brutal shivers;
where those silent waters
flowed a while ago,
flows now a flood—
that peace no more.

***

Why am I?

A Search

Like the Swami[1] erstwhile,
I, too, at moments
feel ties dying.
What do I look up to?
To whom do I go?
The Swami found his answers
from his Master[2]
I, too, must find,
though I know not how.
Till then, it's a search...

Precariously, at moments,
I find myself
at the edges of sanity.
The drop from there
is a long, lost one.
Yet through a Herculean effort
I pull myself
from the edges of that precipice,
and lock my thoughts
in deep contemplation
of my Mother[3].

It re-energizes me.

Thereafter, follows
another search:
to put into words
my understanding,
and that understanding into being.

***

Note: 1. Swami Vivekananda
2. Ramakrishna Paramahansa
3. Mother Mary.

I meditate upon Ramakrishna Paramhansa

The Inspiration

You are standing in a pukur[1]
Come to the sea.
You have the capability to do so.
See where I stand…in the very midst of the sea.
That is where I would like you to be.

When you are afraid of someone,
go very close to him.
You will find he is either mahan[2] or tuccho[3]
If you find him mahan, revere him.
If you find him tuccho, be a mahan before him.

You will have to enter a Masjid[4]
wearing a toupee[5]
as I did;
and take your son,
but only if he so desires.

I said: Jato mauth tato pauth[6]
You may not agree with me wholly now.
That is not necessary.
What is necessary is that when you speak,
speak not as a Christian,

for neither am I a Hindu,
nor is Christ a Christian,
though His followers may be.
When you speak then,
speak as a worshiper—
of Life, of Truth, and of Wisdom.

Be not antagonized by Vivekananda's words.
He spoke what he perceived to be the truth.
You may differ from him.
With time, you, too, will find
that there are some who agree with you
and some who do not.
Thus, is Life: Jato mauth tato pauth.

***

Note: 1. Pond

2. Noble

3. Unworthy

4. Mosque. It was in 1993 that I offered Namaz in a Mosque (in Dhatkidih, Jamshedpur).

5. The skull cap that a Muslim wears while offering Namaz.

6. There are as many paths to Truth as are the beliefs of people.

I meditate upon the Immaculate Heart of Mary

The Inspiration

I will not let you fall
for my love will protect you.
I am your foundation—
your Mother Earth.
Stand firm in me.
The choice is then upon you:
will you be the sword piercing my heart
and add to my pain,
or be the flowers in my heart
and add to my joy?

You worship my Son as your Lord.
Then let me tell you this:
he always walked
at his own destined pace.
He did not permit his pace
to be dictated by men—
even in his missionary life,
crucifixion,
and resurrection.
It was always him and his Father.

This then is my advice to you:

walk at the pace
destined for you.
And walk with love[1].

This then is the yardstick
to make up your mind
whenever in doubt—
Ask yourself:
Will it cause love?
If the answer is "Yes," pursue it.

You will overcome fear,
for I say so;
you will do so with love.
Do everything with love.
Fear then will not exist in you.
Do not let me down.

When you speak, speak with love.
When you are eager to express yourself
and you feel you are absolutely right—
Ask yourself:
Will it cause love?
If the answer is "Yes," speak.

When you desire,
ensure that it is anchored in love—
the love of your Lord.
For desire not anchored in that love

is greed and lust,
no less.
Be then with that love:
That is your destiny, my son.

***

Note: 1. Love, here, is indicative of "redemptive love"—as distinct from "selfish love" or "pampering love" or even the impersonal "selfless love."
Redemptive love (St. John 3:16-17) is motivated by God's glory that is inclusive in nature and the sustenance of A Just Order (Kingdom of God on Earth), within and without oneself (St. Matthew 6:13).

I meditate upon the Crucified Christ

The Inspiration

I do not see thoughts, words or deeds,
I see only the heart:
the purity of desire in the soul.
That is enough for me.
I will receive you wholly in me
and wipe away
the sweat and grime of your tribulations.
So do not worry; I know you.

Do not judge Lily.
In fact, do not judge at all,
for you cannot see the heart.
I see the heart: nothing more is needed.
Her offering I received first,
for she came to me first.
Your offering I received later,
for you came to me later.

Yes, do install my risen form in the church.
It doesn't matter where you place it—
in front or at the back of the church.
I do not dwell in a church
that is simply of bricks and mortar.

I dwell in the hearts of people:
it is there my crib is,
my crucifixion,
and my resurrection.
Go seek me there first.

***

I meditate upon the Risen Christ under the vast open sky

The Inspiration

O man, My heart,
you are from Me:
not I from you.

That path,
strait and narrow,
that leads straight unto Me:
is the path
most acceptable to Me.
And acceptable, too,
is that path,
traversing innumerable turns
through eons of shades and sun,
ultimately leading unto Me.
But then, by the latter,
you lose precious time and will
to live your cross into perfection.

Because "I AM:"
you are.
Because "I AM:"

These paths are.
To you
I have revealed
the understanding of "I AM,"[1]
as also the understanding
of the paths unto "I AM."
But that path upon which
you choose to walk,
is yours:
and so it ought to be.

My Response

O Lord,
I cannot even see
myself
as Your slave:
and yet You exalt me
as Your heart.
I know
that upon each path
I tread,
has a price.
Such is the dignity
You have endowed into "Being."

That path,
strait and narrow,
that leads swift as an arrow
unto You:
is the path
that is acceptable to me.
And acceptable, too,
is the price
to tread upon that path.
O Lord,
to be in shelter
in the hollow of Your love:
is forever the goal of my being.

In seeking You, O Lord,
as seeks the Ganga
the Bay of Bengal,
the yearning in my soul
is born anew...
dancing through this vast stillness.

***

Note: 1. "AM" is the Omnipotence or the Almighty or the Father, and "I" is the Innate Manifesting Power of the "AM" or the Omnipresence or the only begotten Son of the Father.

The Tree

I see the sun on a vast open sky,
its light bathing a tree beneath.
Shortly, I see a snake upon the tree.
As it opens its jaws
I see sharp teeth
and fire flowing out of its mouth.

I see a small, white, beautiful bird
on the ground at the foot of the tree.
Quite suddenly, its beak becomes protruding
large,
and the bird is no longer beautiful.

Then I see dark clouds cover the sky,
lashing rain follows,
and a storm that sways the tree from side to side.
After a while, the rain and storm cease.

Next, I see a yellow flower, a *Kolke phule,*[1]
fall from the tree on the puddle below—
the green sepal turned upward.
I see, then, a drop of water,
like a glistening teardrop,
falling upon the puddle;
and even hear the sound of that drop

as it falls upon the puddle.

Then, I see a gigantic ball of fire,
radiant and magnificent
with circles of light around it,
descend from above and rest above the tree…
flooding the whole sky and earth
with its brilliant light.

***

Note: 1. Kolke Phool: Thevetia peruviana, also known as yellow oleander.

THE MILLENNIUM THOUGHTS

Then I saw Creation as it is—
first was the foundational unity
of "AM" with his "Chosen I,"
and then was the unity of the opposites
from which emerged Being:
moulding creation, akin to a Potter,
from a vast mass of substance
and heat from within...

Of Here And Hereafter

i

When a bud begins to unfold,
it stands apart
and stands alone;
for until the bud becomes a flower
and draws the bees unto itself—
how does its life become fulfilled?

So it is with the soul.

Each soul needs a space to manifest
and each space ought to manifest
the love of Life,
as surely manifests the sun
in the open sky.

Yet the bud that unfolds into a flower
and the sun that ushers the dawn,
has not the power of its own to elect,
nor knows that it is what it is.

It is here that the soul[1] draws apart.

And so in the silence of the night around me
my mind is thrilled with the knowledge
that though the stars have shone

for ages before me,
yet the star cannot be what I can!

ii
The moment of awakening
in the soul
that one comes into being
as an essential and infinite
"elective power,"
for whom the boundary is created
as a derived and finite
"relative power":
not to contradict,
but to enable Life
bring forth fruits of grace
and deepen a Just Order from within—
that moment is for the soul
the beginning of a glorious rebirth!

***

Note: 1. The soul is elective in nature that is governed by the implicit logic of self-determination and choice—in contrast to the cosmos and nature which is relative in nature that is governed by the implicit logic of cause and effect relationship.

Unleashing Individuality

I do not say—
Religion shall perish.

This much I say—
the boundary of Religions
have perished forever,
as the veil of understanding
is lifted from knowledge,
and a singular Wholeness
is revealed to the eyes:
like a great jigsaw puzzle,
harrying one for ages,
is reconciled now into a fruitful Being.

And as the Third Millennium
shall dig its heels into history—
the Unity of Opposites,
the Complete Human Being,
and A Just Order
shall unfold from within that Being.

So where does it lead
the Millennium thinker?

The individual shall deepen
and enrich the group,

as strengthens each finger
the wholeness of the fist,
and the elements come together
to form the atom.

Thus, Group dynamism,
behavior, and development
shall yield the throne
to Individual dynamism,
behavior, and development
in a complete reversal of thinking—
and the inclusive Kutumbakam[1]
shall be deepened and enriched
by the moral-purposefulness
of the elective man[2]

I learnt in History while in Standard Six—
"United we stand,
divided we fall."
Now into the Third Millennium, I learn—
"If divided we fall,
then united we cannot stand."
Thus, if a fist is to be strengthened,
then each finger forming the fist
is to be strengthened first;
for if one of the fingers is weak,
then that weakness is borne
into the wholeness of the fist.

For if the rational Globalization
is to yield place to A Just Order,
then the family, institution, and nation
will have to nurture and unleash
their "Moral Individuality"
into the Third Millennium and beyond.

***

Note: 1. A term in the Ancient Indian Scriptures and Philosophies that means the whole creation is one integrated family.

2. A deeper understanding of the human being from the rational man to the elective man. As the elective man, the human being has the choice to nurture A Just Order in creation in collaboration with his fellow human beings—across class, caste, creed, and nationality.

Logic, not Faith, my Destiny

And so I leave faith for others.

As I read "Cosmos"[1]
and "A Brief History Of Time,[2]
I laugh at the ornamentation of thought
behest of a consistent founding logic—
for if the universe, itself, is uncertain:
how can there be
“A Search for Excellence” for man?
And if existence, itself, is unknowable:
how can there be
“Know thyself" for man?

Around and within me
I experience a wholesome logic
so distinctly existent—
if one seeks a just order,
one would have to desire justice
first and foremost, by choice;
yet, if a seed of apple is sown,
one sees the flowers
grow into fruits with time.
See the distinctive logic?
The first is "self-determining,"
"elective and personal;"
The second is “evolutionary,”

"relative and impersonal;"
the first is "foundational,"
the second is “consequential.”
It is through the marriage of these opposites
that Creation became a "Whole" seamlessly.

If I were to embark on a journey,
I would have to set milestones
leading to a destiny—
for Creation is a journey with a destiny
that is a moral and fruitful existence.
I deny not the primacy
of faith over logic—
for undoubtedly, I know
that it is faith alone
that ushered me into
that glorious and untread
realm of “implicit logic.”
Yet, this too I know
that even the reality of faith
has an “implicit logic,”
an “inherent principle”:
for where the essence of a being
is intrinsically “elective and personal,”
faith is inevitable;
yet, where the essence of a being
is intrinsically “relative and impersonal,”
faith is irrelevant.
So, if faith is to leave its nest

and soar into the sky as an eagle,
and if faith is to break its limits
and align with others into Wholeness,
then surely one needs to know
the "elective logic" of the soul
as distinct from
the "relative logic" of the cosmos.
One speaks of faith,
self-awareness, and justice
when one speaks
of you and me.
Yet one speaks not of faith,
self-awareness, and justice
when one speaks
of the sun and moon.
Or of an apple falling from the tree.

So as I speak
of you and me,
and not of the sun, moon,
or an apple from the tree—
I speak of the journey of faith
into self-awareness and justice;
and of the logic of aligning
that journey
with faith in the One[3]—
who made you and me
an "elective essence"
in His own image and likeness.

And for that “elective essence,”
meaningfulness is primarily by choice
for just you and me.
But for the sun, moon,
or the apple from the tree,
meaningfulness is wholly by causation.

And it’s also for this reason
that for you and me,
co-creators with that One,
time is known
not only by what it brings on board,
but as well by what you and I
give of ourselves to that time.
As for the sun, moon, and the apple,
there is no contradiction,
no uncertainty,
behest as it is of electiveness—
save the general cycle
of cause-and-effect
and a logic that it cannot violate.

It’s not that there is no inter-connectedness,
but that the Law of Electivism
is far superior to the Law of Relativism
in the context of Wholeness;
and in witnessing those “distinctive laws”
my heart rejoices to a deeper understanding:
O Sagan[4],

O Hawking[5]—
you've been denied by that One
you toiled so hard to trivialize!

***

Note: 1 & 4. Carl Sagan, scientist, and winner of the Pulitzer Prize.

2 & 5. Stephen W. Hawking, theoretical physicist.

3. The Supreme Elective Essence or the Father who is the
Creator—Sustainer—Destroyer.

The Unveiling Era

With every passing thought
I find understanding
so easy,
yet living that understanding
so tough.
Why then do I pursue understanding
so vigorously?

But if the Creator has chosen
to be understood by the creature—
more specifically
than a blade of grass
and more transparently
than a gushing spring:
Who am I to hinder that choice?

For if one cannot know the Creator
in spirit and truth,
how can one know oneself
in spirit and truth:
for is not one created
in the image and likeness
of the Creator[1]?
Verily, knowing the Creator
is a gift to the creature—
at the will of the Creator[2].

Yes, in the glow of this Millennium
unknowability has finally been lifted
from over the veil of understanding!
O, let the dawn salute the earth
and the lilies fragrant the sky—
for behold, the elective man[3]
has finally emerged
from beneath that veil—
setting aside once for all
that general perception
that one is but a product
of one's environment.

***

Note: 1. Genesis 1:26-27

2. Matthew 11:25-26

3. Man is a self-determining being, not merely a rational being. So, he can be a rational or irrational being by his choice.

The Holistic Era

i

You and I are really
a will of the Will[1],
clothed in Wisdom[2]
that blends with Nature:
to become manifest here
in spirit and flesh,
in pursuing our destiny
through the changing times.

So to speak of you and I
one has to speak
of the elective will
in hand with the relative wisdom:
for you and I are, at once,
an unparalleled art
of a grain of that elective Infinity
molded in a miniscule cosmos.

Not, then, to depart
as a footprint on sand,
but to leave behind
a heritage to be excelled;
and a model
to serve as a stepping stone,

a today inspiring a morrow—
that is we, you and I.

You and I come into being
as a fistful of time,
spanning from birth to death.
The unknowing
looks at the form and submits:
it is making and breaking
that life is all about…
a momentary play of the Unknown.

Yet, to the faithful is known
that in each fistful of time
is hid
(as hides a fruit-bearing tree
within each seed)
the power to become history:
vibrant and yearning,
striving for the fist to be unfolded.

ii
Go then, I submit, to the Scriptures[3],
rather than Religions.
It is there you will find
the uniqueness amidst similarities,
and, therefore, the Key to the Whole:
by marrying that uniqueness[4];
just as you and I come into being

as unique among equals
yet one in pursuit of Truth:
by marrying our uniqueness—
ethically and purposefully,
with understanding and love.

***

Note: 1. Each soul is a grain of the will or elective power.

2. Each soul is embodied into a unit called the wisdom that is derived from the soul, which is in union with its innate manifesting power called the desire.

3. The various religions are derived from a specific scripture—and not the vice versa.

4. Each scripture has an unique role in the context of A Just Order. It is erroneous, therefore, to contend that all scriptures are the same; the difference being only environmental. It is in the prayerful and intelligent union of the uniqueness of the scriptures that the Whole can be understood.

The Reconciling Era

The era of Peter[1] and Paul[2]
shall exist now
with the emerging era of Thomas[3] —
where abounded earlier
strict compartments of gender-based roles,
shall emerge now
a Holistic Order of a level playing field;
and guiding that Order shall be
the high priestess, Omniscient[4] ,
empowered by the Anointed One.[5]

I deny not a nation
with a constitutional boundary,
yet each scripture shall occupy a space
to fulfill a destined role
in the glory of that Order.
But for that Order, verily,
the boundary of religions
shall break:
as the Shepherd[6] shall emerge
as the center
to gather the universal flock
around Himself!

***

1-3: All three are Apostles of Jesus. Whereas the writings of Sts. Peter and Paul advocated a complementary role for the women in the context of A Just Order—the writing of St. Thomas advocated a level playing field for women in that Order.
4: Holy Spirit.
5-6: Jesus Christ, the Good Shepherd and Anointed of the Father Almighty.

TELCO, A Pilgrimage

Walking with TELCO[1]
I encountered a thought.
We built a fire
to warm our hearts.
In the heat of the moment
the thought germinated
and bore some fruits[2]
that quenched our hearts.

I claimed the fruits,
for I said
the thought was mine…
that thought I encountered
while walking with TELCO.
Ironical, isn't it?

O thinker,
for a pilgrim you are in Life—
return unto TELCO
that which belongs to TELCO
and, if possible,
ten times over…
with love!

***

Note: 1. TELCO (Tata Engineering & Locomotive Company Limited) is currently named Tata Motors.

2. In the Soul-based and Mind-based Philosophy; which I later expounded into Electivism and Relativism-based Philosophy that unites to make up the Whole.

Reunion

As flesh, we meet to part.
As souls, we part to meet.
It is inevitable.

As flesh, we cling to the other
to survive,
by hook or by crook,
and fear overtakes our path.
As soul, we stand apart
to excel,
by dignity and God's love,
and joy overwhelms our hearts.

As flesh, we are born of this world
as Nature's own:
to bloom for a while,
then forever part.
As soul, we are born into this world
as God's own:
to give of our best,
then await reunion[1] with our own…

***

Note: 1. Resurrection of Souls.

Living, A Celebration

You and I, O friend,
are the celebrants of Life,
journeying to perfection
through our births and deaths.

There is time in that journey
for sorrow and joy—
sorrow in the troughs
and joy in the peaks;
one seasons the soul,
the other reveals its glory;
the one without the other is barren,
the other without the one is shallow.

Sorrow is, then,
in the essence of living,
a co-traveller to perfection
that brings to living a rare dignity—
some sorrow
a sense of pride,
and joy in abundance in the time to come!

When life becomes a vicious cycle
of hate begetting hate,
then the Cross, that is Love through Sacrifice,

stands out as the Key to Eternity.
That is why, I guess,
Easter must follow Good Friday.

And so as Easter, the Celebration,
comes only after the Cross—
in becoming an "Easter People"
one upholds, not bypasses, one's cross.

***

Strolling through the Garden of Knowledge

In me, O Life,
let the sorrows be put behind
as puts the sun, the clouds that obstruct it.
In me, O Truth,
let the breath of love flow unchecked
as flows Nature's love into the gardener's toil.
In me, O Way,
let my steps be firm each day
lest I walk not this road again tomorrow.

The true test of Knowledge
is not in its capacity to inform,
for thus it ought to do:
but in its capacity to discern
the good from the evil.
And the true worth of the Mind[1]
is not about knowing and doing,
for thus it ought to do:
but in its capacity to help
the Soul fulfills its commitment.

It is said—
that which limits,
seeks to bind the boundless:

so set it free!
Yet, I see—
in limiting a choice to meaningfulness
is the road to fulfillment,
of that which is boundless and free!

O seeker, until the finite and limit
is derived
from the infinite and limitless
of volition—
there can be no time and space,
no manifestation and multiplication,
no ethical-purposefulness,
nor self-awareness.

Yet to merely make or break a limit
is not the goal of the Soul:
but to expand the horizon of justice
ceaselessly…

And O seeker, all is in Love
for both the Amoeba and the Christ…
the difference being of levels really.
The one, clinging unto itself—
as does the parasite to its feed
and death to its stench:
manifesting the limits of worldliness;
the other, shedding from itself—
as does the wheat from its chaff

and the butterfly from its caterpillar:
manifesting the richness of Truth.
For that which is of the world
clings on to the world,
and thrives in the womb of darkness;
but that which is of Life
returns to its own,
and sheds light on Truth and Darkness.

O Crucifer—
it was enough that I could compose
as I strummed the chords of emotion;
until you desired
that I ought to look at Existence as well.
Then my poetry
entered the Garden of Knowledge,
and witnessed an understanding so deep…
I never dreamt existed!

***

Note: 1. The mind is the exterior agent of the soul, for it embodies the soul and gives it a form. Thus, the mind is always aware of the exterior environment of the soul, and keeps the soul informed of it. The real challenge for the mind is to win the trust of the soul and be a wise counselor.

Destiny

Beyond is the Sun,
before it a storm;
I desire to enter the Sun.
Once again, a gentle David
must come to life
to stem a Goliath,
and a reed-like Peter
to mold himself
into a rock of faith.

I may fail to succeed
but I never fail to try,
for my goal is set in that Sun.
He becomes my will
and the hurdle is split
beneath my stride.
And thus, He leads me on—
beyond the success
that the world can give!

***

Cycle of Creation

i
The Cycle of Creation is about
a journey—
from void to void,
a beginning from and an end into
a meaningful state of rest.
Neither is void chaos,
nor an unknowability;
nor is creation a mere illusion
or a meaningless event
of cause and effect.

The Cycle of Creation is also about
a destiny—
a manifestation and multiplication
of a glorious meaningfulness
leading to A Just Order
by self-determination and choice;
and the implementation
of that chosen meaningfulness,
aesthetically and logically,
by wisdom.

ii
In that Creation,

this body is gifted to me
to be used meaningfully—
neither to be preserved,
nor to be misused;
for embedded in that body
is the spark to be awakened,
that one may join with others
into a celebration of creativity…
and so add to that Glory of Light.

***

A Parting of Love

O Man, who is spirit in flesh,
O Nature, I am your partial being.
Yet lest through the light of the soul
I fail to manifest in truth
the glory and mission of myself,
O Nature, I renounce my right on you—
as did the Mahatma before
renouncing his flesh for truth,
and the Crucifer, some while before,
in disregard to the might of the Jews.

These then are my thoughts, O Nature,
though not that I love you less—
O Nature, you are in worship yourself
to the One that has created you;
why then shall I offer your flowers
for worship in place of me?
Let me dare myself, O Nature,
to offer in worship myself,
as did the Mahatma and the Crucifer
just some ages ago.

The heart is the flower of the soul
for the soul to offer in worship,
and the soul is the tender of his heart
as Nature is the tender of her flowers.

But as Nature is the truth of 'Here'
to accompany the soul in his task—
O Nature,
you were deemed to go no further from here:
that you may implant in the womb of your
creation
the seeds of your own destruction,
so as to return to the soul his freedom,
the freedom for his onward journey…

***

Soul, the Male Power

Never has the earth
strayed from its orbit;
for to be in orbit
is the perpetual role of the earth.
Never has the sun
strayed from its axis;
for to be on its axis
is the perpetual role of the sun.
And so, the earth and the sun
are in perpetual obeisance to Eternity—
through no will,
but by force of nature.

But, O Lord—
Where is the soul's orbit?
Where is the soul's axis?
Yet to that soul you exhort:
"Be perfect as your Father is perfect."
Verily, I salute those elective souls!

You who stress that the soul
is eternally perfect
or there is no proof that the soul exists
are so acutely lucky—
for the Lord has not taken away from you

that veil of unknowability.

***

The Genesis of Genesis

From eternity has been the Will,
before time and space were,
before the desire to uphold life and not death,
and the wisdom to relate death unto birth,
has been the Will—
self-determining and self-existent,
unembodied and unmanifest.

At first, awoke the Will his Desire
from within
to manifest himself;
then derived the Will his Wisdom[1]
from without
to become embodied—
with a zeal to be Complete.

From Will arose the Desire
to begin and to end,
and from Will came the Wisdom
to Be;
for central to Being[2]
is neither Desire, nor Wisdom
but the sovereign of Being—the Will.

Will is the Leader,

Will the Life,
from Will the Whole,
in Will the strife—
husband of Wisdom,
father of Desire,
both good and evil.

Verily, the Genesis of genesis
is the story of Will, the Essence,
emerging as the Holy Being,
with his Sacred Desire
and Holy Wisdom:
of One becoming Three
and of Three becoming One,
in pursuit of A Just Order based on Love.

***

Note: 1. Unlike all other scriptures and philosophies, the Bible is Will-centric–not Wisdom-centric. The Father is the Supreme Will or Almighty or Omnipotent. Creation begins and ends by his choice. Desire and Wisdom emerges from the Will. First, the Will becomes One with his chosen Sacred Desire. This is called "I AM." Thereafter, at the choice of the Will, The Holy Wisdom proceeds from the Will, which is in oneness with his chosen Sacred Desire. The Bible is the Semitic Philosophy of Existence.

2. The oneness of the Will (Omnipotence), the Sacred Desire (Omnipresence), and the Holy Wisdom (Omniscience) is called Being or Holy Trinity.

Hello, Death

Let us adorn this journey
with our love,
so that death—when it comes—is received,
and not ignored as a stranger at the door
shuffling its feet to be known.

He who permitted death
for you and me,
made you my complement
and I, your truth—
as complements the form
the substance.
Then let the form be so rooted
in the substance,
that faced before us as one—
death would have to stand to gaze,
knock to be known,
before separating you from me.

For you and I are the image
of a Great Life,
I knew you
before death was.
So even though death
will set us apart in this journey,

I'll know again your beckon
(through the evening hours of time)
waiting ahead at the Door of that Life—
as waits ahead the shadow
having emerged from her faithful beloved.

O, Mon Ami,
the physical has no uncertainty
for it is denied a choice of its own—
be it the dawn with its glorious birth
or the dusk with its mellowing death.

It is in the spirit that the choice is abode
to be certain or uncertain and confused—
as in the spiritual light of Nanak
or in the spiritual darkness of Hitler.

Then resist, and we must, the death
not of the rose that dies at its hour,
but of the soul that dies through choice
of betrayal, sin, and injustice.

***

To Death a Tribute

Like a child beneath a mango tree
I stand in wait,
as time, the hand of God,
rustles through the leaves
and my people, one by one,
fall upon the earth
in eternal sleep.
It seems I have a tryst with death.
So, unto death, I turn,
to gaze into death in quiet…

If out of Life comes
both, birth and death—
then surely, Life is greater than both,
birth and death.
And if in Life, death follows birth
as in day, dusk follows dawn—
then surely, death and dusk
must signal the close of a cycle.
Life then is the owner
of both, birth and death.
For where a man sows his seed,
his woman conceives
not merely a birth
but a death as well.

Verily, death is writ
large upon my forehead
since the day I was sired
into my mother's embrace.
O, Crucifer—
you restored unto death his grace
by linking death to the Last Judgement
and embracing the cross in living.

So, as I journey through Life—
let me not stand in wait
or flee the face of death;
nor cheat that journey of Life
through quickening the pace of death.

And for each journey of Life is a manifestation
moving from birth to death—
in being alive to a manifestation in me,
I become alive to an allotted time and space
and to death, the end of that allotment.

This, then, is my Tribute to Death—
"O, Great Divide,
for you mold boys into men,
or else are cast aside
as scraps of history.
O, Great Boundary,
you are the witness of Life's journey
into glorious self-manifestation

through the changing time and space.
In saluting you, O Death,
I salute Calvary
and I salute Kurukshetra
in every man's journey.
And if Death be the hour
by which I may journey higher still,
then, O Death,
come at your hour…
I shall not shy from you!"

***

In Deathlessness

i

In my office is a poster
of a Rising Sun—
overlooking the tall grass,
on the banks of a pool,
at the foot of a hillock.

The poster reads:
I believe in Tomorrow.

Often, I have wondered:
"Am I a dreamer?"

Now,
as I look at the poster
and within,
I find my tomorrow
was born in the yesterday,
that has been growing forever
in the fire and stillness
of today.

If this makes me a dreamer,
then shall I not dream on?

ii

Shall I not then also say:
I believe in Today.

For if in the heart of today
is not the yearning
to make tomorrow
a richer day,
then surely today
shall burn itself out.
And if in the mind of today
is not the understanding
that the road to Wholeness
leads through Separateness
and Oneness—
then surely today is yet to awaken.

iii
My tomorrow is set to celebrate
neither only Separateness
nor only Oneness—
but to celebrate, indeed,
A Just Wholeness…
for whose becoming
my today must transcend
the limits of yesterday.

Shall I not then say, too:
I believe in Yesterday.

Faith, emerging from our soul,
that together we shall create
a New Dawn—
keeps our today,
born of yesterday's love,
restless for tomorrow…

***

O, Gujarat

Walking through the dust storm of a summer
noon
tends to blur the mind;
yet, what would defile me:
the dust all over my body,
or the vengeance hidden in my heart?

The ravaged earth of that January quake
did not stoop the head in shame,
as did this bloody March—
when the heart exploded from within
its hidden agenda of hate!

O Lord,
you knew that the Jews knew not
that of zealous ignorance
are terrorists made.
Guide then our hearts to your wisdom.

***

Forbidden Fruit

There is poetry in me
that is God's doing,
attracting by its thoughts
flowers in bloom.
I yearn to pluck
and place in my heart
one such a flower in bloom.

Yet a deeper realization
checks that yearning—
that poetry in me
is of God's doing,
not of my own!
I am but a garden of Truth
where flowers find a cause to bloom.

Fear gathers in the heart,
as dark clouds
in the monsoon sky,
of a derailment by choice.
O poet, let then that flower
bloom in the Lord,
and fight that derailment within!

***

A Tribute

As I saw you breathe your last,
I saw Death bow to receive you
in an embrace that was full of love
beyond all earthly pain.

White was the color of your wedding dress,
and the shimmering glow of your face,
white, too, was the color of your coffin,
and the flowers that adorned your grave.

O Noble Friend,
in the years we lived as one—
I saw in the glow of your flame,
the way to live "The Vow"[1]
in loving faithfulness.

Then grieve no more, O Peter,
for by the prayerfulness
of her love,
you are transformed already
from a poet to a Jesus-thinker.

***

Note: 1. Marriage Vow.

Gathering Mysticism

i

How gently flows the Spirit of God:
it touches the spring
and the woods are filled with flames of forest;
it touches the clouds
and the rivers are moved into swirling waves;
it touches the hills
and the peaks become green in abundance.
But of itself,
the Spirit remains untouched!

Yet, it touches man,
that clod of earth holding the breath of God,
and is itself touched:
for it is in man
where the Calvary lies,
the Kurukshetra, and the Karbala!

ii

Carnal love, no matter how joyful,
can never equal the joy
of Spiritual love—
and so, the former has to die first
in the here and now,
before that white-hot passion
can transform itself into mystical love.

Verily, the death of the former
begins the birth of the latter
in the truest sense.

No one is born to live forever
but to write one's history
before striding 'home.'
It is only on the pyre of carnal love
that mystical love is conceived—
for mystical love arises from a Fire
that is deathless in its thirst for justice.

If then my love for living
is any less
than the flame of that Deathless Fire,
then I am flawed.
Pray then with me, O Noble Souls,
that I may wage a ceaseless jihad[1]
within myself—
InshAllah!

***

Note: 1. A true jihad is the struggle to contemplate within and purify oneself.

Beyond Original Sin

I reject neither a feminist,
nor a male chauvinist—
one seeks not to set aside,
but to reach out
with love and understanding:
for both are manifestations
of a deep commitment—
caught in a vicious cycle
of inadequate reasoning.

And I reject not the fundamentalist—
Hindu or Muslim,
Christian or Jew:
for here, too, is a deep commitment
caught in a vicious cycle
of outdated reasoning.

If indeed I reject,
then it is the covetous will,
a fruit of derailment:
born of the desire to achieve
without the price of morality.

How then can the Meaningful Will
be made
for the vicious cycle to be broken?

I speak not of negation,
or of renouncing in fear:
for Creation is willed
to manifest in perfection.
I speak of a time to be still
in God's own love,
of a time to dialogue
on the holistic logic,
of a time to remold one's Will
with a New Understanding,
and of a New Commitment
to give of oneself unto others.

***

Easter-tide

If the Christmas child fails to grow up
into an Easter person,
victorious and timeless—
but is caught in a time warp
of ceaseless pain and suffering,
caused by injustice—
what then is ‘good’ about Good Friday?

Surely then Good Friday shall be
a futile journey
of a meaningless Existence!

But if the cycle of time
opens at Yule-tide
and closes at Easter tide:
having earned its grit and glitter,
like the steel and gold,
passing through white-hot fire—
then the Cycle of Being
is completed meaningfully
by the soul.

Verily soul—the free will,
a grain of the Omnipotence,
comes into being

not for freedom per se—
but for a journey into excellence,
along with one's cross,
freely chosen…

Happy Easter!

***

Time

Time never returns, they say:
Why should it?
Life became manifest and multiple
not by chance; but by choice.
It is in the faint of heart and unknowing
that gnaws the urge to retreat—
even before the cycle is closed
and truth manifests in completeness.

Time is not eternal—
but begins and ends
with Life desiring in truth
to manifest and multiply.
Nor is time empty—
but akin to a fertile field
awaiting to deliver history
in collaboration with the human race.

And so time flows on,
in waves of peaks and troughs
bound to its tryst with Life—
so often exhorting the richness in us
to lose in spite of ourselves:
a mystical dying to live
in the Calvary of today

for tomorrow's Resurrection!
I knew not time
until I began to know myself.
It is then I knew time
as opportunities-in-motion,
and the destined journey of Causation
at an innate pace.
Today, I fear not death
but of going to the Lord in barren—
for He gave me a worthy mission
and a handful of times to match.

***

Note: 1. Here, Life is used in a specific term, indicating the self-determining Will or the Omnipotence, seeking manifestation and multiplication through creation.

Philanthropy is dead?

So often I am told
that Philanthropy is dead;
what reigns supreme
is Entrepreneurship.

Yet, as I look into Life,
I realize,
that were I to empower another
to come into one's own,

I would have to give space,
of volition,
for the other to grow
beyond my reach—

then surely, I would need
the bountiful heart
of a Mother Teresa and J N Tata,
the philanthropists.

Yesterday gave way to today,
no doubt,
only to give birth to tomorrow's dream
for a higher reach;

for is it not true
that tomorrow's fruit
will be the manifestation of the seed
planted yesterday?

And surely as the fruit
cannot come into being
without the birth pangs
borne by the seed,
the maturity into Entrepreneurship
could not have been reached
without the pioneering rigor
borne by the philanthropists.

And as the seed of yesterday
was the founding sire
of the hope of tomorrow,
so, too, the spirit of Philanthropy
has been the cornerstone
in the journey to Entrepreneurship.

In a deep sense, then—
Does the past really die?
Is not the past
forever present
in becoming future,
in one Cycle of Creation?

***

Akin to a Gentle Breeze

As one journeys forward
from the generalized
to the distinctive plane,
one's hidden,
underdeveloped, and unknown aspects
becomes as magnified
as one's visible,
developed, and known aspects.

In that state of duality,
the hidden,
underdeveloped, and unknown,
tends to veer the focus away
from the visible,
developed, and known—
and even threatens to derail
that journey forward.

In those threatening moments,
when the heart is engulfed in stress,
the presence of a Facilitator,
akin to a breath of gentle, breeze,
helps to remold the Group's thinking
and guide it wisely to its destiny.

***

Of the Desires

The zeal to push the frontiers of time
is so deep in me
that I often get swept off my feet;
sometimes, even derailed.
It is miles and months later
that I see the damage done:
the precious moments lost
and the need to retreat
to be on rail once more.
So often it seeps into me
that it was so much
about so little.
Yet, in growing,
can I deny a movement
between the trough and the peak
as I hasten towards my destiny?

So, in moments of peak
I keep my radar alert—
lest a wayward desire
becomes empowered mistakenly.

***

Of Moral Theology

God desired,
from void into creation,
the sustenance of A Just Order
within and without his Being:
through a purposeful will,
sacred desire, and
a holistic vision
of existence.

The Satan sought to derail
that perfect creation
through manipulating the creature's
immature will,
lack of faith, and
inadequate understanding of existence.
This, in brief, was the clash
between
God, the Holy Trinity,
and
Satan, the rejected evil desire,
at the very start of human creation.

The Original Sin, then,
is a heady mix
of a pampering will,
a reckless heart, and

a distorted understanding of existence—
that permitted the Satan
to achieve a foothold
into human creation.

This, in brief, also
is the challenge that confronts
the People of God
who seek to pursue
that Just Order
within and without their Being…
cutting across boundaries
of gender, religion,
culture, and nation,
through the changing time and space.

Why, then, did God permit a situation
whereby Satan could achieve a foothold
into human creation?
Very simply:
Can one deserve to be free
and yet not be tested
whether one is indeed
moral in one's freedom?
Do we not provide our children
the freedom of education
and yet be tested in exams…
simultaneously?
Was not Jesus, too,

led by the Spirit
at the behest of the Father,
and tested in his weakest hour?
Yet—
Did Jesus fail?

***

Fare Thee Well

I'll come again,
as do the lashing rain
after a scorching heat—
Will you reach out to me?
I'll come again,
as do the dew at dawn
after a restless night—
Will you remember me?

For now, I must go my way
as my destiny beckons me.

As do the gypsy on the road,
so, too, the seeker of truth—
one waits not at the glade,
but seeks out life anew
beneath the sun.

I know not what I leave behind,
save this I know—
I carry with me a Song of Hope
you and I wove
in those years together.

***

Logic of Being

So often I ask myself:
Where do I begin?
From where does anyone begin?
Or, for that matter,
from where did God begin
while still in the state of void[1]?

In the sublime depth
of the Soul, of course:
where lay asleep,
in abandon innocence,
untouched by fear of guile,
the Sacred Desire[2]—
waiting to be awakened,
with gentle love,
to begin a fresh creation.

There, too, lies our beginning—
in the sacred desire of our soul.

Thereafter, it is possible to witness,
step-by-step,
the splendor of creation emerge:
empowered by the zeal of one's soul,
and molded,
ever so skillfully,

by the wisdom of faithful love.

***

Note: 1. The State of Existence before a Cycle of Creation.

2. The Word or Sacred Heart.

The Universe and I

i

Each has a destiny, gifted,
for existence is meaningful
by the choice of the One
who willed it to be so.
Yet, whereas for the universe,
that realm of relativism,
the fulfillment of destiny
is by the impersonal logic of
cause-and-effect;
for you and me,
the image and likeness
of that One,
the fulfillment of destiny
is by the personal logic of
self-determination and choice—
a feat of great challenge and joy.

ii

In creation, then,
there are two Realms
that blend into a Whole,
seamlessly and perfectly:
the supporting Realm of Relativism
that is based on the
impersonal implicit logic

of cause-and-effect;
and the primary Realm of Electivism
that is based on the
personal implicit logic
of self determination-and-choice.

iii
For the human being, a soul,
that is a grain of free will,
the Realm of Electivism
is of prime concern.
Many years ago I asked myself,
"Why am I?"
Today, I reckon
that the universe and our body
are platform and tool
of relativism.
It is on and through
that realm of relativism
that you and I are called
to make our offerings
to the One's goal of creation
of meaningfulness.

Yet, owing to the effect
of the "original sin,"
the nature of human inclination
is always vulnerable to waywardness.

iv

It is to that distinction between
the universe and the human inclination
that Jesus indicates
when he says—
"Take therefore no thought
for the morrow,
for the morrow shall take thought
for the things of itself"
(Realm of Relativism);
"Sufficient unto the day
is the evil thereof"
(Realm of Electivism).

***

Of Time Again

i

I have found time
to be very meaningful and progressive,
yet, equally limited:
for it can only move forward;
neither can it stop,
nor move backward.
Compared to time,
the human person
is so very powerful:
one can keep progressing,
or stop progressing,
or live in the past
while existing in the present
during one's lifetime—
by sheer self-determination and choice.

ii

Time has no choice
but to move on ahead.
Yet, for the human person:
one can be meaningful or meaningless,
progressive or fundamentalist
by one's choice
and level of understanding!
It is for this reason,

freedom and understanding
is the birthright
of the human person—
not of time.

iii

What then is time; and why?
Time is causation
in embodiment,
that it may move
at a pace and way
conducive to conversion
of Creation, step by step,
into an environment of Just Wholeness.
Hence, time is never empty:
but brings in its wake
new knowledge and understanding,
and moments of opportunity;
moving in troughs and peaks
for sowing and reaping
ever new meaningfulness—
exhorting the human will
to fulfill one's destiny
within the span of one's lifetime.

iv

At birth, verily at conception,
the cycle of time opens
for a soul in an earthly body;

at death, the final moment,
the cycle of time closes
for that soul in that earthly body.
It is the time
between birth and death
that the soul is exhorted
to add one's mite
to that Just Wholeness—
the Goal of Creation.
So, through the Cycle of Time,
the contribution of a soul
to the Goal of Creation
is related directly
to the Salvation of Souls.

Many years ago, I wrote:
O Time,
you trod so gently
that I could gaze into Life
more deeply...

***

Cosmos

i
There can be no chaos in the cosmic reality,
no contradiction, nor uncertainty:
for the cosmos, in the ultimate,
is a "relative reality"
that is based on cause-and-effect logic;
and, therefore, not empowered
to deviate from its nature and role.
The chaos in the human reality, however,
the conflict, and uncertainty there,
is the outcome of contradictory human choices:
for the human person,
being an "elective reality"
that is based on the logic
of self determination-and-choice,
is endowed with the power
to be meaningful or meaningless
by choice and the level of understanding.

ii
The deviation in the cosmos
can only arise
where the "elective power" intervenes
in the cosmic functioning:
for unlike the human person,
the cosmos cannot violate

its own nature and role.
The cosmos, thus,
poses no threat to humanity;
the threat to humanity
can be posed
by humanity itself,
or by a still superior elective power.
It is then for humanity to realize
that with "elective power" comes
not only freedom and rights,
but more significantly,
the obligation to be meaningful and just.

This, in the truest sense,
is the essence of individuality.
By nature, then,
"elective power" is superior to
"relative power;"
And the logic of
"self-determination and choice"
is superior to the logic
of "cause-and-effect."

iii
What then is the cosmos; and why?
Let me use imagery.
If I were to manufacture vehicles,
I would need an assembly line
that must move at a pace and way

that is perfectly certain,
rational, and impersonal.
This is the cosmos.
But the self-determining, creative,
and personal power
to create the former
and move oneself
at the pace and way
of that assembly line
is the soul,
the "elective" power.

***

Rose in my Garden[1]: Concluded

She was more than my poetry—
she was a mystical yearning
waiting to be fulfilled,
lighting herself like a flame,
so that I could see Life
more clearly and meaningfully.

In effect, all too often,
I had to raise myself
to her level,
to see that Living is
in the Joy of Giving of oneself
to help the other grow.

In a rare way,
she was that Rose in my life
I had been longing for—
gifted to me
by my Mother[2].

I realize a poet brings out of the heart,

that which one experiences deeply;
yet, the poet is not the doer—
the poet is just the witness
to the doer.

The doer is the one
who upholds oneself,
akin to a candle flame—
to give light to the world
around...

***

Note: 1. "Rose in my Garden," August 1969
2. Mother Mary.

Of Life, Void, Creation, and Being

One who understands not death,
understands not Life, nor birth;
one who sees death to be a lie
but Life to be the only truth,
or, death to be the bitter truth
but Life to be the beautiful lie—
sees not the wholeness of Life.

In Life are three 'states':
the 'State of Void,'
the 'State of Creation,'
and the 'State of Being.'
In a miniscule way,
death is akin
to the 'State of Void,'
birth is akin
to the 'State of Creation,'
and living is akin
to the 'State of Being.'
In that miniscule way, too,
the soul is akin to Life.

Yet again—
the 'State of Creation'
is akin to a day's work;
the 'State of Being'
is akin to manifestation
and multiplication of Life;
and the 'State of Void'
is akin to a moment of rest
after a day's honest work.
Eternal alone, then, is Life
and its innate manifesting power:
that begins and ends
its 'Void,' 'Creation,' and 'Being'
by self-determination and choice,
with love…
For death,
akin to the 'State of Void,'
is both the end and start
of living,
so, if death takes me away this night,
grieve not for me beyond a while:
for death is but a moment of rest,
before I am born into A New Dawn
and a Higher Destiny to fulfill—
till in the Last Judgment[1]
at the Doorway of Eternity,
you and I, O Souls,
are destined to meet again.

***

Note: 1. Mt 25: 31-46 of the Gospels of Jesus.

Death, the Gateway

Let us never forget
that Life is to be lived—
and not to be preserved.

We do not bring a candle
to adorn and preserve it;
rather, we light the candle
that it may give light
to the world around it.

By living its life in full,
the candle in due course,
must burn itself out:
for that is the fulfillment
of its destiny.

It is by this 'meaningful death,'
that one earns the right,
to enter Eternal Life—
for this is the goal of living,
even though it is so painful.

It is again through death,
that Life brings to living
a time-orientation, self-discipline,
and accountability—
for or else living would become
meaningless and undisciplined.

I realize then,
death, too, has a role
in the Salvation of Souls—
just as living has,
in the span of time
between birth and death.

Yet, it is not every death that becomes
the Gateway to Eternal Life—
but only that which is the culmination
of a meaningful living,
contributing to A Just Order.

It is the role of the soul then,
to raise the mortal body
to glorify God Almighty—
by living meaningfully
that leads on to A Just Order.

***

Logic of Living

In one's birth is born
the consequence called death;
but the span of time,
between birth and death
is the present called Living.
It's in the pursuit of A Just Order,
the goal and motive of Creation,
that determines for one
the quality of death:
for if one's span of Living
has been meaningful indeed,
then one's death cannot but
be meaningful, as well.
So, what is Living?
Seeking to become manifest,
with love and meaningfulness,
from within oneself,
so that the manifestation
reaches the farthest person,
in one's birth and thereafter:
is Living.
Honestly, I cannot see,
how sorrow can be the enemy
of human joy;
rather, I see,

sorrow awakens the realization
that joy has to be earned:
for joy that comes without sorrow,
is shallow and meaningless, no less.
Sorrow, I submit, therefore,
seasons one
and makes joy meaningful.
Can there be a Resurrection
without Crucifixion?
The Father Almighty—
the Creator, Sustainer, and Destroyer—
would simply not permit that:
for the goal and motive of Creation,
is to pursue A Just Order,
in one's lifetime.

I guess my greatest
discovery this birth,
has been the understanding
of sorrow and joy,
in the context of A Just Order:
the goal and motive of Living;
and so, relates directly
with Salvation.

***

Freedom, my Birthright

For I was born in the freedom
of a loving marriage,
freedom is my birthright
and I know of no greater joy
than the joy of freedom—
freedom to choose
and so, know myself;
freedom to walk
on the untrodden path;
freedom to question
and contemplate deeply;
and freedom to live
on my own terms.

Yet, for my freedom is embed
in the meaningfulness[1] of Life—
were I to lose that inner meaningfulness,
my freedom would lose
the joy of its authenticity.
My freedom is then not limitless
but limited by my choice to be meaningful,
and not to be wayward.

To me then,
the Source of Ultimate Freedom
is the One who took up his Cross
freely,
and then rose from his death
triumphantly!

***

Note: 1. Morally-purposeful by self-determination and choice.

Logic[1], Dogma, and Maya

To have faith is to believe
the unbelievable;
for it suspends reason.
Yet, faith has a logic,
simple and straight:
There can be no faith
without free will,
without interior freedom,
without self-determination and choice.

Again, there is no scope for faith
in a state of sheer
cause-and-effect relationship.
Hence, doing 'Surya Namaskar'
is as right or wrong
as playing football or cricket,
for mental and physical health:
no more, no less.

Thus, where a faith cannot stand
the scrutiny of logic,
then one needs to question
the worth of that faith.
Logic is not opposed to faith,
but akin to a companion,
that helps one to discern

the worth of one's faith.

If faith does not lead
to works of mercy
and works of empowerment
that leads on to A Just Order
born of love,
then verily that faith
cannot justify Salvation:
indeed 'Solo Fides[2]
itself is unjustified;
read, then, if you will
"Parable of the Good Samaritan"[3]
and the "Yardstick to Excel
in the Last Judgment."[4]
For are not faith and love
built into works—
the very Logic 1 of "I AM"[5]?

Behold, the Third Millennium
has sounded already
the death knell of Dogma and Maya;
and lifted forever now,
the Veil of Unknowability,
from over the Face of Creation:
for that which was hidden and concealed,
by self-determination and choice,
is revealed and given now to Understanding.

***

Note: 1. Implicit Logic.

2. The dogma that faith alone is justified for Salvation; and that no good work is required to accompany that faith.

3. Lk 10:25-37.

4. Mt 25:31-46.

5. The Manifest Righteous Almighty—meaning, the Almighty who chose to be and manifest his innate Righteousness.

Death and Change

You say:
Death is the ugly truth and
Birth is a beautiful lie.
How utterly contradictory!
The reality is:
there can be no death,
without birth.

So, if one desires
to speak on death,
one has to understand, first,
the "what and why of birth?"

So, too, if one desires
to speak on change,
one has to understand, first,
the "what and why of creation?"

Death and change then,
are not inevitable realities:
but the consequence of That,
intrinsically elective and personal,
which seeks to manifest its innate truth,
through a cycle of time
and moral-purposefulness.

***

Essence of Creation

Neither do we come into Being
'empty-handed,'
nor do we pass into Judgement
'empty-handed,'
but each is born with a destiny;
and then with time,
pass into Judgement,
laden with the outcome
of one's choices[1]:
be one a believer,
or, a non-believer.
Let's never even dream
that the human person was destined
to be part of the Evil One:
for God Almighty don't play dice;
but yes, in the ultimate,
He desires and wills
that each one of us
prove worthy
of His magnificent love;
that indeed is the intrinsic nature
of God Almighty:
"One has to earn one's spur."
Thus is the Essence of Creation.

***

Note: 1. One’s works are the outcome of one’s choices: just or unjust.

Of You and I

i
There is a child within me,
who is an eternal inquirer,
there is a man within me,
who has been seasoned by Life:
and is called upon now
to share that seasoning.
Together, I am.

ii
The commonest of reality
between you and I
is that we are uncommon,
yet challenged to be one:
by self-determination and choice,
for the glory of A Just Order,
that is impelled by love.

iii
I didn't have a choice
about my birth,
it'll be the same
about my death;
but in between
it's all about choices[1]:

some yours,
some mine,
and some ours—
hopefully for something
to cherish about…

iv
For you and I to choose
is inevitable:
for it is the state of creation;
it is akin to dying,
for one who is born,
for that is inevitable
in the cycle of time[2].
Yet, none of the two
defines Living.

To make our choices meaningful,
to help others choose meaningfully,
so as to live meaningfully,
in the period of time,
between our births and deaths:
is what defines Living,
and is the challenge
of you and I.

v
A nation and the universe
is all about you and I;

so don't let anyone
tell you different[3]:
you and I,
the living souls,
are the prime cause
for which a nation
and the universe exists.

A leadership that provides,
wings for the able,
and homes for the needy:
shall be called progressively-just.
The rest:
a little here,
and a little there;
a speech here,
and a speech there…

***

Note: 1. Choice is the empowered desire;
the embodied choice is the thought; and
the manifestation of the thought is speech and action.

2. At birth, one's cycle of time opens;
at death, that cycle of time closes; and
it is in the period of time between one's birth and death—that one is given the opportunity to showcase the purpose and motive for which one came into being.

Creation, hence, is very meaningful—in the context of A Just Order.

3. Together with the essential self-determining Commitment ("I Am"), there is also the need for the evolutionary Understanding of the. "Self."

9 789363 31356

Printed by Libri Plureos GmbH in Hamburg,
Germany